Books
of the
Bible

Books
of the
Bible

*With a Succinct Narrative
about Each Book*

JEROLD C. POTTER

A BARBOUR BOOK

© MCMLXXXVIII by Jerold C. Potter

ISBN 1-55748-521-6

 Member
Evangelical
Christian Publishers
Association

Published by   Barbour and Company, Inc.
                 P.O. Box 719
                 Uhrichsville, OH 44683

Printed in the United States of America.

FOREWARD

Over the course of history many men have dedicated their lives so that we can learn God's Word and develop in our spiritual faith. Because of their efforts, today almost every home has a copy of the Bible.

Before the days of the printing press, the Bible had to be written by hand in many different languages. There was a time not too many centuries ago when a copy of the Bible was so rare and precious that many people could not own one. They would walk miles from their village to a church where the Bible was kept chained.

In an effort to encourage more people to read the Bible, John Wyclif (or Wycliffe) became the first, in 1380, to translate all of the books into English. Almost 200 years passed before Miles Coverdale printed the first complete English Bible in Zurich, Switzerland, in 1535.

The Bible, in fact, became the first book to be printed from moveable type. This milestone was accomplished on the press of John Gutenberg of Mentz, Germany, in 1456. Printed in Latin, a copy of this Bible was sold in New York City in 1926 for $106,000, at the time the highest price ever paid for a single book.

As you peruse these brief narratives of the books of the Bible, take a moment to "rediscover" this most amazing book. The journey of the Word of God is only complete if it is embraced by those who possess it.

The Books of the Bible

The Bible was written over a period of 1600 years by more than forty authors. Because God used human authors and their individual styles to write the Bible, the Bible says God's Word was *given by inspiration*, which means to fill or breathe into. Today the Bible is printed in 182 languages.

WHAT IS THE BIBLE?

The name Bible is derived from the Greek word *biblos*, meaning "book." This book is composed of sixty-six separate books originally composed in Hebrew and Greek. The order of these sixty-six books in the

Old Testament and the New Testament is a logical one giving, in general, a consecutive history of mankind—from Genesis to the visionary future of Revelation.

OLD TESTAMENT Comprised of thirty-nine books, the first "half" of the Bible may be broken down in the following manner:

(A) *The law or Pentateuch.* The Pentateuch, derived from the Greek meaning law, includes the first five books: Genesis, Exodus, Leviticus, Numbers and Deuteronomy.

(B) *The historical books (history).* These twelve books are: Joshua, Judges, Ruth, 1 and 2 Samuel, 1 and 2 Kings, 1 and 2 Chronicles, Ezra, Nehemiah, and Esther.

(C) *The poetical books (poetry).* These five books include Job, the Psalms,

Proverbs, Ecclesiastes, and the Song of Solomon. These books are also called the devotional books.

(D) *The prophetical books (prophecy).* Lamentations. Includes *the major prophets* Isaiah, Jeremiah, Ezekiel, and Daniel.

(E) *The minor prophets.* Hosea, Joel, Amos, Obadiah, Jonah, Micah, Nahum, Habakkuk, Zephaniah, Haggai, Zechariah and Malachi.

NEW TESTAMENT Written in the Greek language, the second "half" includes twenty-seven books and may be divided into four parts. These books are broken down in the following manner:

(A) *The Gospels.* Matthew, Mark, Luke, and John.

(B) *History.* The Acts of the Apostles—
the book of Acts.

(C) *The Epistles.* Includes twenty-one
books. The first thirteen are called
the *Pauline Epistles* because they
were written by the Apostle Paul:
Romans, 1 and 2 Corinthians,
Galatians, 1 and 2 Thessalonians;
Ephesians, Philippians, Colossians,
and Philemon (the *Prison Epistles*);
1 and 2 Timothy and Titus (the *Pastoral Epistles*). The next eight are
called *General Epistles* because
they were written by other apostles:
Hebrews (author unknown), James,
1 and 2 Peter, 1, 2, and 3 John, and
Jude.

(D) *Prophecy.* The book of Revelation,
also known as the Apocalypse of
St. John, is prophetical.

The Old Testament

(1) **GENESIS** means beginnings. This book tells the story of the beginning of the world and the first man and first woman.
- a) Their names—Adam and Eve
- b) Their children—Cain and Abel, first two sons
- c) It tells of Noah who built the great Ark and lived in it during the flood.
- d) It tells the story of Joseph and his brothers.
- e) It tells of Abraham, who trusted and obeyed God.
- f) Isaac and his sons, Jacob and Esau.

(2) **EXODUS** means going out. The book tells about the children of Israel or the Is-

raelites who were taken as slaves and were captives in Egypt for 430 years. It tells the story of Moses at birth and as the man who led the Israelites out of Egypt. Exodus also tells of the Ten Commandments.

(3) **LEVITICUS** is the book of laws. It gives many laws to govern the Israelites. Many of the laws are ways in which the people should worship God. The commandments are included.

(4) **NUMBERS** contains certain chapters that record a sort of census taking (counting the people). Moses and Aaron numbered the people of the different tribes. Other stories include sending out of the spies, bringing water out of the rock, death by fiery serpents, and healing through the serpent of brass.

(5) **DEUTERONOMY** tells how people should act toward one another and toward

God. These laws teach kindness, honesty, and reverence. The story of the death of Moses is told, and of the curses and blessings of mankind.

(6) **JOSHUA** is the first of the group of books called books of history. Some thrilling stories include the Israelites crossing the River Jordan on dry land; the fall of Jericho; the death of Joshua who led the people so bravely and wisely through all the adventures in this book.

(7) **JUDGES** continues the story of the Israelites in the Promised Land. It is named for the rulers who were called judges. The judges whose stories we know best are Deborah, Gideon, Jephthah, and Samson.

(8) **RUTH** is the beautiful story of a loyal young woman named Ruth who would not leave her dead husband's mother, Naomi. Ruth finally married a wealthy relative

named Boaz, the great grandson of Ruth and Boaz was David.

(9) **1 SAMUEL** tells of the foundation of the Hebrew kingdom. Some of the stories well loved in this book are of Samuel for whom the book was named; Saul, the first king of Israel; David and Goliath; the friendship of David and Jonathan; David sparing King Saul; Abigail the peace-maker; and the death of King Saul and his son Jonathan.

(10) **2 SAMUEL** is the story of Israel under the rule of King David. In the first chapter David laments over the deaths of Saul and Jonathan. David was a warrior and had delivered the people from their old enemies, the Philistines. David built a strong capital at Jerusalem and brought back the Ark of the Covenant that had been captured by the Philistines. This book tells of David's kindness to the crippled son of

Jonathan and David's rebellious son Absalom.

(11) **1 KINGS** tells in the first verse that King David was old and stricken in years. When King David died, his son Solomon reigned in his stead to the day of his death. In this book we have stories of the building of the great temple; the prophet Elijah and wicked King Ahab and the dreadful death of Jezebel, Ahab's queen.

(12) **2 KINGS** tells of many kings and many wars. One of the most thrilling stories is of Elijah taken to heaven in a chariot of fire and Elisha given his place as a prophet. Here are many stories of the deeds of Elisha, as he went about teaching; the story of Naaman, the Syrian, and the helpful little captive Hebrew maid; finding the Book of Law and, at last, the sad story of the destruction of Jerusalem and the captivity of the people.

(13) **1 CHRONICLES** retells that part of the history of the Hebrew people that is given in 1 and 2 Samuel. Many of the stories are told in both places, although in different words. The first nine chapters of the book are given to genealogies, or tracing the ancestry of families. Then there are many beloved stories, such as the death of Saul and Jonathan, David's mighty men, victory over the Philistines, bringing the Ark of the Covenant to Jerusalem, the old age and death of David, and Solomon made king.

(14) **2 CHRONICLES** covers much of the history of the Hebrew people that is told in 1 and 2 Kings. We have stories of the wisdom of Solomon, building of the Great Temple, the grandeur of Solomon's court, and the death of Solomon. There are stories of many kings, some good, some bad, the destruction of Jerusalem, the people carried into captivity, and the find-

ing of the Book of Law.

(15) **EZRA** is named for Ezra, the priest and scribe, who taught the people and helped finish the temple. Ezra continues the story of the Jewish people that was told in the books of Chronicles. The Jewish people had been taken into captivity and the book tells of their being allowed by Cyrus, king of Persia, to go back to Jerusalem to rebuild the temple and worship God as they had been taught.

(16) **NEHEMIAH** tells more of the story told in Ezra of the captive people who went back to Jerusalem. Nehemiah begins about eleven years after the story of Ezra ends. It tells of Nehemiah, cupbearer to the king of Persia, who heard from a visitor from Jerusalem that the wall of the city was broken down and the people were miserable and in danger from their enemies. Nehemiah, with the help of the king, went

back to Jerusalem and rebuilt the wall and taught the people to obey the laws that some of them had broken.

(17) **ESTHER** tells the story of a lovely young Jewish woman who was chosen by the king of Persia to be his queen.

(18) **JOB** is the first book of the poetry group. It is the story of a man named Job who, although he lost his wealth and his sons and daughters, and was stricken with a terrible sickness and abused by those who pretended to be his friends, still believed in God's goodness, and was not angry with God.

(19) **PSALMS** is the hymn book of the Bible. This is the longest book in the Bible and contains 150 sacred songs, many of them written by King David. Some psalms are so beautiful that for thousands of years God's people have loved to praise Him in

the words of these songs. One of the best known is the twenty-third Psalm or the Shepherd's Psalm.

(20) **PROVERBS** is a book of wise sayings and good advice. Most of these sage verses were written by King Solomon, the son of David. The book says a great deal about wisdom and tells us that the fear of the Lord is the beginning of wisdom.

(21) **ECCLESIASTES** is a beautiful poem in which King Solomon looks back over his life and tells what he thinks about it. He has gained wealth and power and wisdom, yet he has done many wrong and foolish things. As he remembers, he often repeats, "All is vanity." This book gives us many proverbs and words of good advice somewhat like those in the book of Proverbs.

(22) **SONG OF SOLOMON** is another

beautiful poem by King Solomon, the son of David.

(23) **ISAIAH** is the first of the group of five books called major prophets or greater prophets. It is the wonderful preaching and teaching and visions of the prophet Isaiah, carrying the message of God to the people of Israel and Judah. He pleads with them to turn from their sins, and promises them good and happiness if they do right, and terrible punishment if they do wrong. In this book God gives the promise of His Son to be the Savior of the world.

(24) **JEREMIAH** gives the teachings of the prophet Jeremiah. He saw the people worshiping idols, doing wrong things in the temple, and even the priests leading the people into wickedness. He was brave enough to preach in public places, and before kings, against the sins of the people, although he knew his life was in danger.

Through Jeremiah God promised to forgive the people if they would be sorry and turn from their wrongdoing. The promise of the coming of Jesus given in this book says, "He shall be called the Lord our Righteousness."

(25) **LAMENTATIONS** was written by the prophet Jeremiah. The punishment promised the people for their sins had come and Jerusalem was destroyed, as we learned from the books of the history. In these sad and beautiful poems called Lamentations, Jeremiah tells of his grief and urges the people to turn to God for help in their time of trouble.

(26) **EZEKIEL** is named for the prophet Ezekiel. God spoke to Ezekiel through many visions, as He did to other prophets, and Ezekiel often taught by parables. A priest, who was carried away from Jerusalem with other captives, Ezekiel declared

that the people should be punished for their idolatry and their many sins by being carried away as captives. However, he promised that they should sometime go back to rebuild their cities. This book promises the coming of the Prince. The prince was Jesus who was born nearly 600 years after Ezekiel told of His coming.

(27) **DANIEL** is a book of teachings and prophecies so wise and deep that Bible scholars for hundreds of years have studied it and still felt that they have not gained all its knowledge. Daniel is also a book of stories so wonderful and interesting that one never tires of hearing them: the brave captive boy, Daniel, who dared refused the rich food and wine ordered for him by the king; of the three young princes thrown into the fiery furnace, but unhurt; of Daniel in the den of lions, and of the handwriting on the wall.

(28) **HOSEA** is the first of the twelve books called the minor prophets, or lesser prophets. The first words of this book tell that it is "the word of the Lord that come unto Hosea." Hosea lived and preached long before the city of Jerusalem was destroyed, but he tells that this punishment shall come to the people if they keep on in their wrongdoing. God says through Hosea, "O Israel, return unto the Lord thy God; for thou hast fallen by thine iniquity."

(29) **JOEL** tells of a time of terrible trouble when a great army of insects destroyed the grain, fruit trees, and vines. There was no rain and even the beasts of the fields mourned because the rivers were dried up and there were no pastures. Joel pleads with the people to turn to God and ask Him for forgiveness and help. When the rain comes again he says, "Rejoice in the Lord your God." He promises that God shall drive away their enemies and "be a

refuge unto His people."

(30) **AMOS** was written by Amos, a herdsman, who became a prophet because he knew that God had given him a message for the people. Amos saw the people who pretended to worship God but were dishonest and cruel to the poor. He told them that for their sins God would punish them, that they should be taken away captives out of their land. At the very end of the book Amos promises that they shall come back to their country and build their cities once more and live in them.

(31) **OBADIAH** is a short book of only twenty-one verses. In this book the prophet Obadiah tells in anger of the people of Edom who, although they were relatives of the people of Israel and Judah, sided with their enemies. They watched strangers carry away the people of Jerusalem as captives and were glad. They even stood

in the crossway to prevent their escape and stole their goods when they were in trouble. Obadiah declares that the Edomites shall be destroyed and the Israelites shall be destroyed and the Israelites shall return and be victorious.

(32) **JONAH** is the story of a man who tried to run away from God. Jonah was sent by God to be a missionary to the great wicked city of Nineveh. Elements of the story include Jonah trying to run away from the work God had for him to do; the danger into which he came, the wonderful way in which God took care of him; Jonah's missionary work and how it came out.

(33) **MICAH** begins with these words, "The word of the Lord that came to Micah." The prophet Micah reproved the people because they worshiped idols and were unjust and dishonest. He told the princes and the rulers that they hated the

good and loved the evil. Micah said that God would punish them for this by giving them up to their enemies. In time He would gather together those that were left and bring them again to their own land. Micah gives the promise of the coming of Jesus and tells that He shall be born in Bethlehem.

(34) **NAHUM** is the prophet Nahum's vision of the terrible destruction of the powerful enemy of his people, the great city of Nineveh. He calls the kingdom of Judah to be thankful, for the wicked shall no more pass through, he is utterly cut off. Then the prophet tells his vision of the terrible army as it poured in and destroyed the great and wicked city of Nineveh.

(35) **HABAKKUK** expresses the prophet's sadness because of the sins of his people and the punishment that God will send them through their enemies, the Chaldeans.

Habakkuk warns the Chaldeans that God will punish them, too, for their cruelty and greed. This book has only three chapters and all of the third chapter is a beautiful prayer hymn written by Habakkuk.

(36) **ZEPHANIAH** tells that one of his ancestors was King Hezekiah. Zephaniah warns the people who think that God will neither help His people nor punish them. Zephaniah says that neither their silver nor their gold shall be able to save those who do not obey God; that their enemies shall conquer and destroy their cities. Besides the warnings to those who will not give up their sins, this book gives beautiful promises of those who are left after the punishment has come to the nation, and are sorry and ask God's help.

(37) **HAGGAI** tells of the time of the book of Ezra, when the people who had been carried away as captives had come

back to live in Jerusalem. The prophet Haggai complained to the governor and to the high priest that the people had built their own houses, but did not build the Lord's house, the temple, for only the foundation of the temple was finished. God's message came through Haggai that the people should go up to the mountain and bring wood and rebuild God's house. The governor and the high priest and the people obeyed God's command. They began work on the temple and God said, "I am with you."

(38) **ZECHARIAH** urges the people who had gone back to Jerusalem to finish the work of rebuilding the temple as did Haggai. The prophet Zechariah had eight visions that were explained to him by an angel. Every vision was a message of courage to the people to tell them that God would bless them in their work. This book gives the promise of the coming of Jesus

and in one place foretells Palm Sunday.

(39) **MALACHI** is the last book of the Old Testament. The prophet reproves the people for their wrongdoing because the priests themselves were leading the people into wickedness; the people were having too much to do with the nations what worshiped idols; and they were not bringing the offerings that they should bring to the house of God. Malachi urges them to do right because God loves them and tells them that God will surely punish those who disobey Him.

THE NEW TESTAMENT

This is the part of the Bible written after God sent His Son to live upon the earth. It is God's message of His great love for us through Jesus.

(1) **MATTHEW** is the first book of the New Testament and the first of the four books called the Gospels, or the good news, because they tell of the story of Jesus. Matthew one of the twelve apostles helps the Christian Jews to understand that Jesus was really the Savior who was promised so many times in the books of the Old Testament. The prayer that Jesus gave that we call the Lord's Prayer is in the sixth chapter of this book. The story of the wise men is told in this Gospel, but not in the others.

(2) **MARK** was written by a man of that name, who was a special friend of Peter, one of the twelve apostles. Mark does not tell the story of Jesus as a baby or a child, but begins the story of Jesus as a grown man. Mark wished to teach those who read this book that Jesus is the Son of God.

(3) **LUKE** was written by a physician. Many of the best-loved stories are told only in this book. Some of these are the angel's good tidings and the shepherds' visit, the boy Jesus in the Temple, the good Samaritan, the prodigal son, raising the widow's son, and healing the lepers. The Apostle Paul called Luke "the beloved physician."

(4) **JOHN** is the last of the four Gospels. John, like Matthew, was one of the twelve apostles and wrote of those things that he had really seen and heard. This book also begins with Jesus as a man. John does not tell all of the stories of Jesus that the oth-

ers tell, but he tells of the love of Jesus and of the Father who sent Him and why God gave His Son to the world.

(5) **ACTS** is the history of the acts or deeds of the apostles after Jesus returned to heaven. This is the story of the beginning of the Christian church and the church's birthday, named the Day of Pentecost. In the first part of the book one reads of the brave deeds of Peter and in the latter part, the wonderful stories about Paul. The story of Stephen, the first Christian martyr, is in the book. This book of history is believed to be written by Luke, who wrote one of the Gospels.

(6) **ROMANS** is the first of the group named Pauline Epistles. Epistle is another word for letter and the thirteen books in this group are letters written by the Apostle Paul to Christians in different places. Paul, the great missionary, had long wished to

visit the church at Rome. He could not go at that time, so he wrote this beautiful and helpful letter to take the place of his visit. Paul tells his readers that righteousness is a free gift from God.

(7) **1 CORINTHIANS** is the letter written by Paul to the Christian church in the city of Corinth. Paul had received bad news of this church. Its members were quarreling and doing many other things that Christ's people should not do. Paul wrote this letter to help the Christians in Corinth correct their faults. The thirteenth chapter of this book is like a beautiful poem and is often called the "Love Chapter."

(8) **2 CORINTHIANS** is the second letter written by the Apostle Paul to the Christian church in the city of Corinth. The members of this church have had Paul's first letter and are trying to overcome their wrongdoing, about which he wrote. Paul

tells them of the offering the churches are giving to the poor in Jerusalem and asks them to help.

(9) **GALATIANS** is a letter written by the Apostle Paul to all the Christian churches in Galatia. Many of the members of these churches were not Jews but were Gentiles. Some men had come among these churches and stirred their members up against Paul and his teachings by telling them that they must keep certain Jewish laws. Many turned from Paul and believed the new teachers, and the church members were quarreling among themselves.

(10) **EPHESIANS** is another letter written by the Apostle Paul. Wise people who have studied this epistle think that it was a circular letter intended to be passed around and read in several churches. When Paul wrote this letter he was a prisoner in Rome,

awaiting trial. This is a beautiful letter in which Paul urges the Christians in these churches to live in such a way as to be worthy to be followers of Jesus.

(11) **PHILIPPIANS** is a letter written by the Apostle Paul when he was held prisoner in Rome. The Christians in Philippi had sent a messenger to him with gifts and when the messenger was ready to return , Paul wrote a beautiful letter for him to take back home. Paul thanks his friends for their gifts and urges them to be true followers of Jesus. It is often called the Epistle of Joy.

(12) **COLOSSIANS** is a letter written by the Apostle Paul to the members of the church at Colossae. Paul had heard that a false teacher was teaching the members of the church at Colossae things that were not true. He wrote this letter urging these Christians not to believe this wrong teach-

ing, but to know that Jesus is all powerful in heaven and on earth. He gave some plain rules to grown folk and to children to help them live lives pleasing to Jesus.

(13) **1 THESSALONIANS** is the first letter written by Apostle Paul to the members of the church in the city of Thessalonica. This letter was written while Paul was making his missionary journeys and before he was a prisoner in Rome. Paul praises the Christians at Thessalonica and tells them that they are a good example to other Christians. He says he does not need to say anything about brotherly love to them because they are taught of God to love one another.

(14) **2 THESSALONIANS** is another letter written by the Apostle Paul to the Christians at Thessalonica. He tells these Christians that he thanks God for them. He is proud of them because they are pa-

tient and true through persecution and trouble. Because Paul had taught that Jesus is coming again, some were expecting Him soon and were not doing their work. Paul tells them that no one knows when Jesus will come, that everyone must do his work, and that those who will not work have no right to eat.

(15) **1 TIMOTHY** was a letter written by the Apostle Paul not to a church but to his dear friend, Timothy. Timothy was a young teacher and preacher whom Paul often took with him on his missionary journeys. In this letter Paul gives Timothy some good advice on Timothy's Christian life and work in the churches.

(16) **2 TIMOTHY** is the second letter written by the Apostle Paul to the young man, Timothy. Paul is like a father to Timothy and calls him his beloved son. Paul feels that he is soon to be put to death

for his faith in Jesus and begs Timothy to carry on the work faithfully as a workman who has no need to be ashamed. He asks Timothy to do his best to come to him before winter. Part of this letter is a loving farewell to a dear friend.

(17) **TITUS** is a letter written by the Apostle Paul to his friend and helper, Titus. Paul had left Titus on the island of Crete to look after the churches there for a time. This letter, written back to Titus on the island, advises him about his work and teaching among these churches.

(18) **PHILEMON** is a short letter, just a note, written by the Apostle Paul to a friend named Philemon living in the city of Colossae. Philemon's slave, named Onesimus, had run away from home and had gone to Rome, where Paul was a prisoner. There in Rome Onesimus, the slave heard Paul preach and became a Christian.

As he was about to return to his master, Paul wrote this letter for Onesimus to give to Philemon. The letter asks Philemon to receive Onesimus, not as a servant, but as a beloved brother as if he were Paul himself.

(19) **HEBREWS** is the first of the group of eight books called the General Epistles because they were letters written not to any one person or church, but to a large number for more general reading. It is a letter written to the Christian Jews, or Hebrews. The letter shows these people who had kept the old Jewish law that Jesus' way of living takes the place of the old law. The writer encourages them to be brave and true in persecution and trouble and to do the good and kind things that the followers of Jesus should do.

(20) **JAMES** is written by the Apostle James to the Jewish Christians. James tells

these Christians how people who have faith in Jesus should act toward one another. He teaches them that unless they act in the Christian way they are not followers of Jesus. James also tells the readers to be a doer of God's Word.

(21) **1 PETER** is the first letter written by the Apostle Peter, one of the twelve apostles who were with Jesus. This letter was written to the Christians who were being cruelly treated. Peter comforts these Christians and urges them to be patient and remember that Jesus suffered, too, "that he might bring us to God." He tells them to live good lives among their neighbors who are not Christians, to be obedient to rulers, patient in suffering and loving to one another, that when Jesus comes again they may be glad with Him.

(22) **2 PETER** is the second letter written by the Apostle Peter. He knows that

he has not long to live and he wishes to remind the followers of Jesus of the things they should believe and do. He warns them of the false teachers that will come and urges them to be true to their faith. He tells them that no one knows when Jesus will come again and that they must be careful that they are ready for Him.

(23) **1 JOHN** is the first letter written by the Apostle John, who was one of the original twelve apostles. This letter tells, just as it told the followers of Jesus so many hundreds of years ago, that God sent His Son because He loved us: that if we would be companions with God, we must accept the gift of His Son for ourselves; we must love Jesus and love one another. The apostle tells us that we cannot keep God's commandments unless we are loving and kind to one another.

(24) **2 JOHN** is the second letter written

by the Apostle John. It is a short letter of
only thirteen verses. The apostle says that
he does not write a new commandment, but
"that which we had from the beginning,"
that we "love one another." He warns
against those who teach that Jesus Christ
has never lived as a man on the earth and
advises to have nothing to do with these
false teachers.

(25) **3 JOHN** is a short letter written by
the Apostle John to a friend he calls Gaius
the beloved. The apostle expresses wishes
for Gaius and praise and joy for his good
deeds. He asks Gaius to receive kindly
certain Christian teachers who are travel-
ing about. He says that he hopes soon to
see Gaius and speak with him face to face.

(26) **JUDE** is a letter written by the
Apostle Jude and is the last epistle or letter. Wicked men were among the Christians and this letter is written as warning

against them. Jude reminds the Christians of the punishment that God always brings to those who turn away from doing right. He urges the Christians to do right themselves and to keep others from following the ways of wicked men.

(27) **REVELATION** is the last book of the Bible. The strange and wonderful prophecies in Revelation were visions given to the Apostle John when he was an exile on the Isle of Patmos. For hundreds of years, scholars have studied this book of prophecy; its great promises have given courage and comfort to the followers of Jesus all over the world.

AFTERWORD

Jerold C. Potter continues to teach the Word of God with such faith, power, and love that the message reaches the heart. Jerold's heart's desire is to see people grow and develop in God's faith and authority, so that they may be free from the devil.

THE WORD OF FAITH AND POWER PRISON MINISTRY was founded by Jerold C. Potter several years ago. In this ministry, Jerold teaches in the youth authority with boys who have been incarcerated. He teaches Bible truths to the boys using parables with school subjects such as geography, science, English, and history.

For additional information write to:

JEROLD C. POTTER
P. O. BOX 2732
LOS ANGELES, CA 90051

NOTES

NOTES

NOTES

NOTES